Dylan and Maria
A True True-Love Story

As recorded by
JANET SANDERS
(her mother)

To Dylan and Maria, of course, without whom this story couldn't exist.

To God for the gift of being a writer.

To the Holy Spirit for the clarity of thought, memory, and imagery to write 10,000 words in two 5-hour sessions in June 2019.

ISBN 978-1-958054-00-0

In the winter of 2020/2021, in the middle of the COVID-19 Pandemic while we were quarantined in separate households: me at the farm, Dylan and Maria in their first apartment, I did some phone interviews where they shared parts of their story and perspectives that I didn't previously have. Those have been added to the original manuscript.

. . .

Benjamin and Natalie are not their real names. Everyone else's names are correct. Events and details are as accurate as memory could recall and others could corroborate.

TABLE OF CONTENTS

Dylan and Maria

PROLOGUE
BEFORE THE FIRE

Maria and Dylan first sort-of met in August 2018 when they shared a first-hour facilitated independent study class in Engineering at Limestone Community High School. She was taking Architecture I and Dylan was in Mechanical Engineering II. She was a junior; he was a senior.

Maria never mentioned Dylan then, and I don't know how much he noticed her. It would have been at least in passing–she was one of only two girls in the class and always wore a hat. She was the only one in the school allowed to wear a hat because it helped protect her eyes from the UV light that would accelerate her vision loss from Stargardt's Juvenile Macular Degeneration. She was also quite beautiful. She had waist-length chocolate brown hair, intensely blue eyes, and she dressed with an iconic self-assured style unlike anyone else at the high school. So I'm sure he at least noticed her.

Dylan's comment later was, "I knew who she was, and

that she was dating Benjamin. I had a girlfriend. I just didn't go there. Once you get past about 14, you don't crush on every pretty girl you see. But she was always really cute." So nothing was lit at first sight.

In September, Maria told her Dad and I that she was planning to finally join FIRST Robotics. She always intended to be an Engineer, making childhood drawings of designs to improve things in her world–like wipers for backseat car windows so she could see outside when we drove in the rain. She had considered joining FIRST Robotics when she was a freshman and again as a sophomore. But she likes to have time and energy to do things properly.

Her freshman year was full of new high school experiences, marching band, and performing in the school's Variety Show as a solo act–singing and playing piano. It included being in the Limestone's Madrigal Dinner Brass Quintet, and continuing her Irish Dance lessons. She didn't want to throw a wrench into her already-full schedule by taking on something that she didn't know if she would like, how hard it would be, or how much time it would take. She was also emotionally coping with the vision loss she had been told at age 13 was going to be part of her future. But by her junior year, she was ready to add something new. Dylan had been in FIRST Robotics since his sophomore year and was now co-captain.

When the introductory pre-season started in October, Maria didn't talk much about anyone who was at the meetings. She didn't really know anyone, and mostly was trying to get her bearings on the activities. And she didn't like it. She was on the Software sub-team and was struggling both visually and with the learning curve on the software. She doesn't like not knowing what she's doing, and she doesn't like feeling she's not adding value. FIRST Robotics was full of both.

She did have fun on Design and Competition day one Saturday. Her team won handily, and the design was heavily her idea. The competing team's device that was soundly trounced was heavily Dylan's design. They both have clear memories about the competition day but only vague memories of each other.

In November, anyone interested in participating on the FIRST Robotics Argos competitive team had to submit an application. Maria was not planning to apply.

"I won't be picked anyway. I'm too new at this and I don't know what I'm doing. Besides, I don't really like Robotics, and I don't like competitions. I just like to do stuff. I'm not applying."

I back-channeled an email to Mr. Walser, her Engineering teacher, and asked him to share with Bradley Krone, the FIRST Robotics Argos team Lead Mentor, that Maria was not going to apply and we were making no headway convincing her. I thought some encouragement from them might make a difference.

Bradley's response was something like, "OMG!!! What does she mean she isn't applying?! Of course she'll make the team. She's one of the best ones we have!"

Encouragement was forthcoming. They let her switch sub-teams and told her what an asset she would be to the Argos team if she would please just apply. She did. They accepted.

PART I
TWIGS ARE GATHERED

Argos began five-times-a-week meetings in January with the goal of designing and building a robot in six weeks. You have to average 10 hours of participation out of 18 possible hours per week to qualify to go to competitions. The first week Maria told me which days she was skipping since going every workday was not required. I corrected her. Not going was only acceptable with a valid excuse no matter the lower limits of participation set by Bradley and Mr. Walser. Monday was excused for her Irish Dance class, but Tuesday, Thursday, Friday 6-9pm and Saturday 9am-3pm were required by us. She was not happy.

She came home from meetings pretty stressed.

"I don't understand most of what they're talking about. It all just goes over my head and the other guys nod and discuss back like they all know what gear ratios are, and all sorts of other stuff. I don't even know what the words mean, much less how it applies to the problem. And I don't know the tools. Somebody asked me to go get them something and I didn't even know what it looked like. I probably wouldn't have been able to find it in the dark, messy drawer of tools anyway even if I knew what I was looking for. Mostly I just stand around, and sometimes try to be useful by putting things away and straightening up."

On a team with a bunch of engineer-minded teenage boys, Maria really didn't understand how useful that was to Mr. Walser and Bradley!

She did start to talk about the kids she was getting to know. I heard the names Chad, Caleb, Kyle, Ryne, Billy, Nate, Brendan, Noah, and Dylan.

One evening, as she was describing the different personalities, she said, "Dylan is really nice. He reminds me of George (her brother) and looks kind of like Robert Downey, Jr." She immediately pulled up a social media picture of Dylan with his girlfriend Natalie, dated Christmas Eve 2018. "Natalie is super sweet. She was in my English class last semester. They've been dating a long time and are so cute together."

I noted how she stared at the picture. Noted the tone in her voice when she said he reminded her of her brother. Noted that he had a girlfriend. Noted how long she stared at the picture of them. So, I'll sit back with the popcorn, watch what unfolds, and see what of that matters.

In February, she said she still didn't like FIRST Robotics, but at least she enjoyed spending time with the kids that were there. She was one of six girls on the team.

One girl was the eighth-grade younger sister of one of the guys. The other four were a gaggle from another high school she said everyone referred to as "The Girls." The Girls hung together, looked pretty, and didn't do much.

Maria was not one of The Girls. She was one of the Team. So the kids she was enjoying her time with were all guys.

"But I definitely don't want to do Mechanical Engineering. Small parts that move and won't work if they aren't aligned just right drive me crazy!"

We talked about how learning what you don't like is as valuable as learning what you do like–sometimes more. If that was all she got out of her experience, plus some new friends, it was worth it.

Her Dad and I continued to reassure her that until she'd been through the whole process, she needed to withhold judgment. At the end of the season, when she could look back at the journey, then she would be in a position to decide if the work had been worth it.

One night she came home all excited that she had been of real value that evening. A square pipe and a large gear had to fit inside the robot housing. No one else's hand would fit in the tube to hold everything in place while it was fastened together.

"At least I was useful today, Mom. It's a good thing I'm on the team. They'd have been stuck if I hadn't applied and been picked. All the guys' hands were way too big to do it!"

We laughed about Robotics becoming "the right place at the right time" for her, and how life could make you useful for the most unexpected reasons in the most unexpected ways.

One night she came home talking animatedly and laughing about a ridiculous conversation that had happened. It started with a group of the team tasked with figuring out various ways a robot might grab a ball. Rube Goldberg ideas abounded. Maria gave a generic, simple idea. Nate dismissed the idea saying, "Our robot won't be unique if we did that."

Maria, in frustration at all the fancy, unworkable ideas that had been offered, responded with a touch of sarcastic wit, "What would make our robot unique would be to attach a ferret to it to grab the ball." Dylan, who was not part of the group, happened to overhear the comment and volunteered that such a critter would be a "grapple ferret." Much silliness ensued.

As Maria reconstructed to me who said what, she commented that verbal jousting with Dylan was as easy as wordplay games with her brother.

"We just bantered back and forth like I do with George. It was so much fun!"

They both remember it as their first real interaction. Dylan said later he had thought she was shy and reserved because she didn't talk a lot, and found her fun banter and quick wit unexpected. She was not who he thought she was. At a bridal shower game 3 years later when asked what he noticed first about Maria, his answer was emphatic. "How incredibly smart she is. She didn't have any trouble keeping up when we were going back and forth about the grapple ferret. And it went on for a long time."

A few weeks later she brought home the Argos uniform. The team is sponsored by Caterpillar Tractor Company whose corporate colors are a deep yellow and black. The pants she brought home were the most hideous bumble bee-striped black and yellow pattern we had ever seen. While the pants are normally worn with a black shirt, CAT also provided a black and yellow checkered flannel shirt. I insisted she put the two pieces on together. So she squished her girl-curves into the straight-cut cargo pants, added the flannel, pulled her long hair over her face like Cousin Itt of The Addams Family, topped it off with the Argos ball cap, and hid in "fashion shame." The clothing had obviously been selected by engineers. We all just roared. I have pictures.

The competition schedule was sent out: Central Illinois Regional in late March, Central Missouri Regional in early April, and Worlds in Detroit in late April–if they qualified. Worlds conflicted with her Junior Prom.

"I'm not going to say anything to them now, Mom, but if we make it to Worlds, I'm not going. If that means I'm not on the team next year because I ditch them, so be it. I'm not missing my Junior Prom. I already have my dress."

I didn't argue.

As competition season was coming up, there was a bit

of a dilemma about Maria's role. She couldn't see the matches well enough to perform the usual first-year job of tracking how the other robots performed (Scout), and Bradley told her she also wouldn't be Human Player. She didn't know exactly what the Human Player did or why that seemed to be a big deal. Mostly, she wanted a support role in the background that she could manage. She told Bradley she didn't care; she just wanted to be as useful as she could be to the team.

As Bradley weighed options for the various jobs at the competitions, he talked to Dylan about the choices. Dylan was his first pick for Human Player, but Dylan had missed too many build sessions and practices. His after-school job at the local hardware store had kept him from attending enough FIRST Robotics meetings to qualify for the position. It was a harsh consequence for being a responsible young adult, but not unfair.

As Dylan swallowed his disappointment, he caught sight of Maria who was tweaking something on the robot. He offered his opinion that he thought Bradley should give it to her. "She's worked really hard, and she's really good. I think she's earned it."

When positions were announced, Maria was Human Player. She didn't appreciate at the time the honor of the position–or the adrenaline rush it would provide during competitions. As co-captain Dylan was part of the Pit Crew, which made sure the robot was ready for competition and fixed things that got banged up during matches. Between matches Maria and Dylan would be hanging out in the Pit together, along with the rest of the Pit Crew and Pit Crew Mentors.

The first competition was the Central Illinois Regional at Bradley University in Peoria, March 22-24. Her dad and I took the day off work to attend and watch her be Human Player. It was so fun! And it turns out wearing those Argos pants was a status symbol at a FIRST Robotics competition. The team was well-known as one of the best and had been to Worlds multiple times.

Maria told me coming down to the Pit Area to see all the robots was part of the experience. So after one of the matches her dad and I found our way down to their spot. I stood back for a few minutes just watching all those nerdy guys in their bumble bee pants and safety glasses. She fit right in with her hair pulled back in a messy bun wearing her own bumble bee pants and safety glasses. When she noticed us standing to the side she stepped over and gave me a big hug.

"Being out there on the field as Human Player was just amazing! Oh my gosh! That was way better than sitting in the stands being a Scout! When we got back here I was just shaking–I never knew anything could be like that!" She gave me another hug, and then proceeded to point out who was who of all the boys she had been chattering about for the last couple of months. "And that one", she pointed, "that one is Dylan. He's the one who is just like talking to George. He even looks kind of like George. And Tim (her brother-in-law). He's super nice." And she continued to stare at him.

Noted.

After the competition, the kids were supposed to grab some dinner and head back to the high school for a debriefing session. Dylan offered that Maria could join them for the dinner break at Thanh Linh, a Thai restaurant just down the street. Maria didn't know where we were to ask permission, and it was only a short break before they were supposed to be back to the high school. She didn't want to be late and didn't know our plans, so she declined.

We went back to the house, and she grabbed a quick peanut-butter-banana sandwich before heading back up to the high school. When she got there, the guys were finishing their take-out. Ahhh! She didn't think about that as an option. Next time she would know the drill.

Maria noticed that Dylan had ordered Thanh Linh's Crab Rangoon, which she loved, and she said so. Dylan offered her his last piece. One of Dylan's best friends and co-captain, Noah Schultz, gave Dylan an incredulous look and said, "Hey–I just asked you for that and you told me 'no'!"

Dylan replied, "That's because you're a bum."

Schultz retorted, "Yeah, but you never share your food with anyone!"

Teenage boys can be a bit territorial about their calories. Dylan just shrugged.

When I picked Maria up later I asked how the debrief session went. She talked a bit about that, then relayed the conversation about the Crab Rangoon.

"I don't know why he gave it to me and not Schultz. Schultz is one of his best friends. But it was very sweet of him."

Noted.

The next day was Saturday, day two of the competition, and the two of them started talking more. Lots of silliness between them about ceremonial burial salmon and Viking funerals, and an animated discussion amongst the team about the physics of slapping a chicken hard enough and long enough to cook it. One of the guys from another team nearby kept hanging around the Argos Pit. He was very awkwardly chatty and engaged Noah at length. At one point the kid leaned over to Noah, and said loudly enough for everyone in the Pit to catch, "I hear your team has hot girls."

Schultz glanced over at Maria and looked distinctly uncomfortable. Maria turned around and visibly plugged her ears to whatever Schultz replied. Dylan heard the comment and remembers thinking "Well, there is at least one!"

The team took first place at the competition, qualifying them for Worlds. Prom or Worlds? Prom was no longer the easy answer, but Maria opted she would wait until after the Central Missouri Regional to make her decision.

PART II
A SPARK IS STRUCK

The Wednesday after the competition, Maria's dad Bert, her older brother Jimmy, who owns his own game company, and I were leaving for the game convention Adepticon in Schaumburg, Illinois, about two hours north of us. Jimmy and his family lived with us in a multi-generational household on our farm, and Jimmy's wife, Gina, was staying home with their two girls: Samantha, who was seven, and Melany, who was three.

Before leaving, I told Maria that while it was reasonable to ask Gina to take her to Robotics on Thursday evening at 6, it was not reasonable to ask her to pack the girls up and go pick her up at 9pm. "Almost everyone there will be coming back to Bartonville. You have to find a ride home or stay home."

Gina took her to Robotics, but there was a miscommunication between the two of them about the pick-up: Gina had told Maria she could pick her up if it became necessary, but Maria misunderstood her to mean she was definitely returning unless Maria told her otherwise. Maria didn't have pockets in her outfit, so set her phone aside in her hat during practice, and didn't see Gina's desperate texts and missed calls trying to verify whether Maria had found a ride. When Gina didn't get any answer, she called other family and friends to try to arrange a pickup for Maria.

At the end of the evening, Maria looked at her phone and hit panic mode as she read through the missed texts. The last one was that a family friend could pick her up, but it would be a bit. Maria looked anxiously around the thinning group of people. She asked Emma, a mentor, about a ride, but mentors were not allowed to give rides to students.

Dylan heard her asking and offered to take her home. They both say neither of them thought anything about it. She needed a ride, and he had transportation.

Thursday March 28, 2019, 9:00pm turned out to be a date and time to remember.

As they headed to his car, Maria was tired, stressed, and near tears. She fumed to Dylan about all the confusion. He responded with something that included the word "exponential" and Maria turned it into a pun about logarithms, which she had to explain because he was too mentally drained from his day to catch it. Okay, that was a little awkward.

Into his car they settled. As Dylan drove her home, they started talking about books: *Lord of the Rings*, *Mortal*

Instruments, *Harry Potter*, *Dresden Files*, and others. They found they had the same views on several series they had read in common, and they started sharing about the ones the other hadn't read yet.

At one point on the drive, Dylan experienced one of those "out of phase" moments. We've all had them. When suddenly time seems to slow to a near stop and a part of your brain processes milliseconds of details as though they were minutes. Think of the scene in *Pride and Prejudice* when Mr. Darcy and Elizabeth have their first dance, or *The Greatest Showman* when Phillip Carlyle sees Anne Wheeler on the trapeze that first time. The world paused for a moment—and contained only Maria.

After Dylan dropped Maria off at home, he spent a good portion of the next 30 minutes trying to decide how long to wait before sending her a Snapchat friend request. "Need to wait at least an hour. Don't send her anything yet. She'll think you're a weirdo. Don't send anything yet. Just wait a while. Wait at least an hour. OK. Still waiting." And after 30 minutes, "Oops! Finger slipped. Oh well, I guess it's sent!"

During that time, Maria was fixing a snack before heading to bed. When she got upstairs, she opened her phone and saw the request. Her reaction was, "Oh, he sent me a friend request! That's fun–he's really nice!"

They proceeded to text for the next three hours.

Maria always texted and talked to me when I was out of town. I didn't think anything about not getting a text on

Thursday night. I knew it would be late on a school night when she got home. I didn't really think about it on Friday when she didn't text when she got home from school or in the early evening. Sometimes she waited to hear from me that I was free. So at 7:30pm I sent her a text:

Mom: Back at the hotel.

Maria: New friend between yesterday and today.

Mom: Really???!! Do tell :D

Maria: Dylan Livingston, the guy in the Pit. He gave me a ride home yesterday. Talked about books the whole way. Got a friend request on Snapchat and have pretty much been talking since. Half of it completely ridiculous, the other perfectly normal.

"Ohhh!" I exclaimed aloud, as I read the text.

Bert heard my exclamation and immediately asked "Anything wrong? Everybody OK?"

"Everything's fine." I responded. "Just a text from Maria. Give me a minute."

I recognized in that one text what had just happened. It

had happened to me on March 15, 1977 at 10:15am in the Guidance Office of Limestone Community High School when I met her dad.

I texted back:

Mom: Sweet!

Maria: We are very similar as far as mannerisms are concerned. And humor. And seemingly interests. It's like talking to George only not my brother.

Mom: That's awesome!

Maria: Yep. Plus we have the same first hour.

Mom: That will be fun on Monday. It's just funny how relationships can suddenly shift gears from someone I recognize to someone I know.

Maria told me later she found my last comment very odd, but chalked it up to weird old people talk. I was just trying to catch my breath.

I read the exchange to Jimmy and Bert. Jimmy's

immediate reaction was, "Holy sh*t–that sounds like you and Dad!"

The kids are very familiar with our high school love-at-first-sight story. Although it took us about 4 weeks to really understand what happened that day. Well, it took me that long, anyway. I was the one who needed to choose between my long-term boyfriend and my future husband–at least, I needed to choose once I remembered my boyfriend existed, which took me 3 days.

When we got home on Sunday night, Maria plopped on the couch and between incoming and outgoing texts with Dylan told us about the last 70 hours in 45 minutes. I'm not sure she took a breath. It included:

> "We texted until 1am on Thursday and finally stopped because we knew we HAD to get some sleep"

> "In one of the texts he said he was really into Magic. I wasn't sure what he meant by that–I mean, was he into card tricks, or trying to tell me he was Wiccan, or whatever else that meant?, so I sent back 'Magic?' and he said, 'It's a card game. You wouldn't know anything about it.' So I sent back, 'Oh, Magic the Gathering. I know Magic. I have my own deck.' And he sent back 'WHAT???!!!' And I sent back, 'Yep. A friend of my brother's is really into Magic and made it for

me. I've never had a chance to play it, but I have it and it's mine.'"

"We agreed to stop texting earlier on Friday and agreed to midnight, but then it was suddenly 12:30, but we did better last night. Last night at 10:30 he said we should probably get some sleep, but I told him I didn't have any place to be until 3 in the afternoon so I could sleep in and he said he didn't have to be anywhere until 10:30 so he could sleep in as well. We did stop at midnight though. We're working on dialing it back to about 11. We decided that was a pretty sustainable time long-term."

Note that Maria's 3pm activity on Saturday had been to go with her current boyfriend and his mom to shop for some clothes for his job interview. The absurdity of talking nonstop to her new "friend" until midnight and having an outing the next day with her boyfriend quite obviously did not occur to her.

During that outing Maria remembers thinking, "I wonder what Dylan's doing. I should text him. No I shouldn't." Then she did anyway.

They had been texting earlier until she had to leave, and they had signed off agreeing to text again that evening.

Dylan remembers, "I gave her crap about texting me again because, you know, that didn't last very long."

Maria defended herself saying, "When I got to Benjamin's house, his mom wasn't ready to leave, and he was playing a video game. I was bored. And I decided I didn't care if it was 'inappropriate'. I wanted to text you."

> "Dylan's going to Bradley University (which is local to us) in the fall, so he'll still be around. And we talked about how next year if I end up at a college in Wisconsin, that's OK because he has a car and loves road trips, and will just come see me there."

Note again the unrecognized absurdity of the conversation. Jimmy's response the next day when I relayed it was, "What?! Aren't they both dating someone?!" My response was, "Not for much longer!"

She finally stopped to take a breath, noticed the time, and headed up to bed. Bert and I just sat in dumbfounded silence for a few minutes before I could manage a "Well!"

Bert's response was more fun. Shaking his head and staring straight ahead he said, "I have never, ever seen her that animated about anyone. Ever." A long slow sip from his glass of bourbon. Then to me, shaking his head again, "Not even Santa Claus!"

PART III
SMOKE RISES

The next 3 days passed with ordinary interactions with the current significant others and friends, and furious texting back and forth in the background: a lot of random facts about themselves, and a lot of "the question game" as they got to know each other.

Dylan was trying to work out how to manage this unexpected complication in his life. "I had lots of 'Oh sh*t, I already have a girlfriend!' Not sure what this is, but it's a thing. Not sure what kind of thing. Not sure how to navigate this without causing an issue with Natalie."

Maria up front told Benjamin she had found a new best friend and he needed to get over the fact that it was a guy. Maria also talked to her friend, Jessica, about Dylan.

"It's just fantastic talking to him. It's like I just found my best friend!"

Jessica was not at all sure this was a good idea. She worked with Dylan at the hardware store, and the two of them didn't exactly get along. There was no active animosity, but they both found the other mildly irritating. Jess was a chatterbox who could be a little dense, and Dylan didn't always have full patience for her, which Jessica took as a bit arrogant. Besides, Maria had a boyfriend. Benjamin, Maria, and Jess had all attended the same grade school, and they spent a fair amount of time hanging out together.

Maria reassured her, "Dylan and I had a whole conversation on Friday about who we were dating, and how things were going on that front, and that we were happy with our relationships, and we're just going to be good friends. This is just fantastic friendship material, and they'll just have to get over it because we're just good friends and it's wonderful."

Dylan couldn't make Robotics on Tuesday, but on Thursday, April 4, he took Maria to Robotics and brought her home. Earlier in the week, Bert had told Maria that he could help Dylan apply for an internship at Caterpillar, so Maria invited him to come inside to discuss it. It was a good excuse to meet us as well.

Dylan was obviously and understandably nervous when he came in. He sat on the edge of our piano bench and was visibly trying to calm his chattering leg by rubbing it. We had full sympathy for his situation, and did our best to be open and welcoming. Bert and Dylan discussed the internship and Maria sat on the couch, grinning like the Cheshire Cat. Business attended to, so I suggested to Maria that she show Dylan around the house.

The kids' friends long ago christened our old farmhouse "The TARDIS," a Doctor Who reference, because it looks deceptively small from the outside but has gotten quite large on the inside from numerous additions to the original structure. It's kind of an experience to experience it, and we frequently give newcomers a tour.

The first stop on the tour was the bookshelf wall in the hallway. Books being core to both of them, they paused for a while, both pointing out various titles, which gave me a minute to soak in this very first visit.

I was very sure this evening would become part of our family history. I was very sure I was meeting my future son-in-law for the first time. I also knew Dylan and Maria didn't know.

I tried to be casual and not just stare at the two of them interacting. I partially succeeded. Dylan remembers knowing I was watching them, but said it didn't feel weird. Just warm and friendly. About 15 minutes for the tour, and they landed back in the dining room with everyone, ending with a look at family pictures on the dining room walls.

"Seeing the inside of her world for the first time explained a lot about her." Dylan said later. "It all just seemed to fit with who she was."

A snack of cheese, crackers, and grapes, and it was getting very late. Dylan acknowledged he needed to get going. I was in the kitchen at the counter between the kitchen and dining room. Maria and Dylan were on the dining room side of the counter, a little aside from where everyone else was randomly standing. I saw him open his arms, palms up for a few moments as he stood in front of her. Maria says she didn't hear him the first time he said, "hug?" So she responded, "What?"

"Hug?"

"What?"

"HUG?"

"OHHHH!" and she threw her arms around his neck in a full-body, heartfelt hug, hugging with her whole soul. He hugged her back.

First Contact.

When the embrace ended, she stood numbly in place, later commenting, "Everything tingled like I'd touched something electrical and got zapped." Dylan stepped, or I should say, stumbled, backwards a step. He looked like he'd been struck by lightning.

I will never forget the look on his face. It was like looking at one of those cartoon characters after it's been struck by lightning. Blink, blink, blink. You could almost see the smoke curling up from the top of his head.

After a few moments, he saw me standing there and put out a trembling hand for me to shake. "I-I need to be going now."

Maria had told me earlier that she had warned Dylan that I hug, and there was at least a 50/50 chance or better that I would hug him when we first met. Grinning, I stepped forward past the outstretched hand and gave him a hug. As I hugged him, I heard him mumble incoherently to himself, "Oh. Yeah. Right. Hugs. I like hugs." I let go, and he stepped back and pretty much bolted for the door.

As he opened the door to step out he mumbled something like, "Well it was very nice to meet everyone. I'll see everyone again sometime I guess."

To which Bert responded, "We'll see you tomorrow, remember? We're going to the Central Missouri Regional."

"Oh. Right. Yeah. Well then. See you tomorrow." And he was gone.

After Maria left to go upstairs, Bert and I burst out laughing. It was so fun to have witnessed First Contact.

I said, "I'm not sure he was safe to drive when he left here. He will smell the scent of her hair and feel that hug all night. I'm not sure he's going to be able to sleep!"

For Dylan's part, he remembers just sitting in his car numbly for a few minutes, trying to un-fry before he started driving.

About 10 minutes later, just long enough for Dylan to have driven home, Maria came back downstairs. "So Dylan wants to know if it's OK if he picks me up in the morning. Since we have to be up to the school so early for the bus to Missouri, it will save you having to take me."

Well, that's one way to spin it.

"Sure, that's very thoughtful of him." I grinned in reply.

She texted him back. Then, "He wants to know if it's OK if he picks me up a little early so we have time to stop at McDonald's and grab some breakfast for the trip."

"That sounds like a very reasonable thing to do." I answered, grinning from ear to ear. "Tell him thank you for thinking of it. What time will he be picking you up?"

More texting. "He says around 6 or 6:15."

"That sounds fine." I replied.

Maria waltzed out of the room, and when she got out of earshot, Bert and I howled in delighted laughter again. The bus didn't leave until 7, and they didn't need to be there until 6:45.

As Dylan drove to pick her up Friday morning, his excitement was split between getting to see Maria again and the adrenaline of heading to a Robotics competition. Significantly less nervous than the night before, he remembers thinking, "Well, I got a hug. It couldn't have gone too badly."

He was running a bit late–more like 6:20 than 6:00. The first of many "a bit late"s, one place where they are yin and yang. Maria is always prompt, so she was ready and waiting in the living room. She ran outside as soon as she heard his car coming down the quarter-mile gravel drive, so he didn't come in.

Off they went for breakfast at McDonald's. Maria ordered pancakes and a biscuit and gravy. He got a bacon, egg, and cheese McMuffin–his usual. Dylan recalled, "We had this whole conversation about how she does sweet breakfast and I opt for a savory breakfast."

Maria added, "Then I called him sweet. He said he

wasn't, and I should take it back. I repeated that he was sweet and threw a sugar packet at him. He threw it back at me and called me sweet. So I threw it back at him and repeated that he was sweet."

The sugar packet was tossed back and forth until it was time to go. The shtick was repeated at the Missouri Regional and at Worlds. They still have the original McDonald's sugar packet.

PART IV
THE TWIGS CATCH

It was a short drive over to the high school parking lot to get on the bus. They got on, and found an empty seat to sit together. Several of the guys teased them about it. "This is not a big deal. We're just friends!" they insisted. Chemistry is hard to hide, but the protestation was accepted at face value. For the moment.

Everyone settled into the usual kids-on-a-bus-trip pattern: initial energy eventually giving way to quiet monotony. Maria was reading the book *Fantastic Beasts and Where to Find Them*. Dylan hadn't read it yet, so she brought it to share during the weekend. Dylan mostly played on his phone. They talked some, but mostly they shared a quiet, companionable silence with a mutual feeling of "all's right with the world." Along the way Maria fell asleep on his shoulder. Dylan had to fend off some additional good-natured grief from several team members who took advantage of a golden opportunity to harass him.

The competition was being held at the local high

school in Columbus, Missouri. While the arena area for the stands and competition was huge for a high school, the designated Pit area was barely adequate. The Pits were so small and so hot; it was miserable. They all suffered it together.

In a later conversation, Maria said, "When we were testing the robot arm, we had to have people stand in the aisle to be sure no one walked by or they'd get clocked. I had to stand on top of the robot dolly to stay out of the way. It was nice I could fit there."

"Mostly, she just likes to perch." responded Dylan. "I told her she needed to be careful or she might fall off. So I should stay close by just in case. It was sort of true. She *could* have fallen off." He grinned.

Friday afternoon, Bert and I were in the stands and watched Maria be Human Player again. On Friday evening when their team was done for the day, the kids came up to the stands to watch the rest of the events. We were sitting on the top row and watched them come up the stairs, Dylan in the lead with Maria and their teammate Chad following. Dylan picked a row and slid in. Chad stepped in behind him. I saw Dylan turn to see that it was Chad next to him and not Maria, and he frowned slightly. I could just hear him thinking, "Dang. I didn't plan that very well." They all sat down.

I could see Dylan and Chad talking, and I could tell Maria couldn't hear the conversation. She kept leaning in to be included. Finally she stepped down to the row in front of them, and slid in until she was directly in front of Dylan. Dylan brightened considerably at the updated arrangement.

I assumed the conversation between Dylan and Chad had been about robotics. Later Dylan corrected me. "I was telling him to MOVE. He knew I wanted to sit next to Maria. He just grinned at me and was like, 'Why? Why should I move?'" Maria was clueless about the content of the conversation, and had also assumed they were talking robotics stuff.

Now directly in front of Dylan, Maria turned around to join the conversation. As the three of them started conversing, Maria looked up and saw us about 4 rows straight back and jumped up to come and say hi. While she was talking to us, I saw Dylan glance backwards to see Maria standing with her back to him, and I watched as he very nimbly hopped himself down to the row she had been sitting in so that when she came back he would be sitting next to her. He and Chad exchanged a look, and Dylan grinned slightly. Dylan says additional verbal harassment was also exchanged. Maria returned to her seat a few minutes later and smiled broadly as she registered the uptick in her circumstances.

Once the events were over for the day, everyone headed out. On the way to the hotel, there was a general discussion on the Argos bus about going swimming. Maria and Dylan agreed that it sounded like fun, so after a quick change in their respective hotel rooms, they met again at the pool. No one else was there. There was a rule that if guys and girls were together there had to be more than 2 people present. They considered their options. The pool was in a pretty public spot in the hotel with big glass windows looking into the adjacent, populated workout room. They decided that it counted and got in the water.

They spent the time swimming back and forth across the pool, chatting and floating until curfew approached. They agreed on the way back to their rooms that they would change quickly then meet back at the elevators to say good night.

Dylan remembers, "It was the first time I saw her squirrel mafia t-shirt which is a fantastic shirt, and she was wearing her fuzzy white turtle & duck PJ pants. She was *very* cute."

It was almost curfew so there was just time for a very quick, albeit awkward, hug. Maria scampered back to her room, and Dylan turned to see Chad standing at the door of their room grinning from ear to ear. He had watched the exchange. As the harassment began, their other roommate, Caleb, received a video call from his girlfriend who wanted to introduce one of her girlfriends to Chad. The rest of the night was a kind of rock/paper/scissors of mutual harassment.

Saturday morning brought some good matches for their robot, and at the lunch break everyone was excited about the potential to repeat the win they had at the Central Illinois Regional. It was a beautiful sunny day, and lunch was set up outside in a grassy area next to the school. Maria and Dylan found a spot to settle for lunch with a group of teammates. As kids finished eating, several availed themselves of the open space to toss around a Frisbee someone had brought. Dylan declined to join, though he occasionally competed in Disc Golf tournaments.

Maria and Dylan were content to stay where they were, companionably enjoying the warm sunshine. Maria stretched out, using Dylan's thigh as a comfy place to rest her head.

Somebody ran past and winged a piece of American cheese at them which landed on Dylan's chest, barely missing Maria's face. Dylan picked it off and returned fire at the back of his retreating teammate, grinning broadly as he hit his target at 30 feet. "HA!" Dylan exclaimed.

The cheese Frisbee and exclamation caught Mr. Walser's attention, and he noticed Maria using Dylan's leg as a pillow. "That's not professional," he asserted. "Knock it off."

Maria sat up, slightly annoyed. They weren't doing anything. It wasn't like they were a couple. They were just friends. Oh well. It was time to go in anyway. Neither of them yet recognized the chemistry between them for what it was, even as others were noticing.

Later that afternoon, Mr. Walser was sitting near me, and we chatted a bit. He was hoping to get back by 1:30am on Monday morning. I replied my husband and I would leave after the awards, but since we didn't have to load a trailer we should be home on Sunday by 11pm. "And I won't have to go get Maria. She'll have a ride home."

"Dylan?" Mr. Walser asked with a nod. It was more of a statement than a question.

"Yep," I answered. And we both grinned.

When the day's matches were over, the team was in a good spot in the rankings. In good spirits, everyone exited the school arena and headed to dinner and the hotel.

When the kids got back to the hotel, Maria and Dylan decided to take the last part of the evening to play a game of Magic the Gathering. They had both brought their decks. A deck of Magic cards isn't like a standard 52 card deck of playing cards. Each card in a Magic deck is individually selected from thousands of possible cards. Some cards are better than others, and some cards are made to work especially well with certain other cards. Building a deck is a bit of art and a bit of science. Winning a Magic game is partially how well you play, but also how good the cards in your deck are, how well one deck plays against another, and a smattering of luck.

Dylan had built the deck he brought and had been playing for years. Maria's deck had been given to her by her brother's friend. She had never played, and needed some help with the rules. Game over: Maria won.

As they were packing the game up, Billy came over to them. "So, are you guys a thing?" he asked bluntly.

The question caught them off-guard.

"NO!" they both exclaimed. "We're not a 'thing'. We're just good friends."

"OK, if you say so," Billy replied, giving them a sideways look. "But just to let you know, people are starting to talk."

They realized others around them were listening to the exchange and were also giving them odd looks.

The ride up the elevator was quiet. They did the now-customary quick hug good night and headed to their respective rooms. It didn't take but a few minutes for the texting to start.

"Everyone seems to think this is a thing. Is this a thing?" Dylan sent.

Maria answered, "If things were different. In a theoretical world that doesn't actually exist, would you be interested?"

A few tense heartbeats waiting for technology to communicate his answer. "Yes," he replied.

Maria's heart pounded and she suddenly felt a bit light-headed. She took a few deep breaths before she answered back, "If this might be a thing, maybe we should talk about some big stuff. If there are deal-breakers, it would be good to know before this goes any further."

Dylan agreed.

They were now playing a high stakes game of questions. Maria sent questions. Dylan answered. Then Maria texted back her answer to her own question. How many kids do you want? Where do you want to live? What about religion and faith? What do you want to do in life? Where do you see yourself in 10 years? It went on for some time. Maria told me later, "He had the perfect answer to every single one of my questions."

By the end of the conversation, they decided they should pull back and take some time to think about where this was going. It was a lot to take in. They both felt they should give themselves and the other some time to think about it. So they agreed to step back for the rest of the competition, and give each other some breathing room.

When Bert and I got back to the competition location on Sunday morning, Maria came trouncing up the stands with Dylan right behind.

"Dylan and I played Magic last night, and I won!"

I caught just a glimpse of an uncomfortable shadow cross his face, but he grinned.

Maria added, "That deck Collier built for me was really good. I don't think Dylan was expecting my deck to be that good."

Dylan nodded. "She played really well, and she does have a good deck."

A hug hello/goodbye to my daughter and off they headed to the Pit area. Neither gave any indication of the previous night's conversation.

They spent a pretty miserable Sunday morning trying to "give each other space" in the small confines of the Pit, talking to other people, and trying not to interact. They gave up by lunch. Neither was interested in "space."

In the match after lunch, the competition suddenly went sideways. An opposing robot aggressively and illegally rammed into the Argos robot, breaking it.

Back in the Pit after the match, the mentors scrambled to fix the robot before the next match. Looking frantically through the parts box, the Lead Pit Mentor came up empty for the most important broken part. The part was on the spare parts list, but it was not in the spare parts box. Time, space, and tempers were short. Bradley ordered all non-mentors out of the Pit.

Maria commented later, "I can handle pressure just fine; temper not so much. I was OK getting out of the Pit."

Dylan replied, "Her response is flight or turtle. My response is 'do.' I was pissed I got booted along with everyone else since repairing the robot was part of my job on the team."

They came up to the stands together and sat down. Absorbed in companionable angst and frustration, they were oblivious to everyone and everything around them. I didn't know what was going on, but I could see the intensity between them.

It was time for Finals. The Argos robot was literally stuck together with duct tape. When it was all over, they took 2nd place. In most situations, that would have been a good showing. But the first-place team should have been disqualified for breaking their robot, so everyone was fuming.

The bus was loaded up with tired, aggrieved teenagers who had a 5-hour bus ride ahead of them. Maria and Dylan sat in the middle of the bus with most of their friends behind them. As the ride got underway, everyone settled down, and a game of Werewolf started up. Several people asked them to play. Maria was exhausted from the long, stressful day and just wanted some down time and sleep. Dylan was not interested in leaving his seat with Maria, so he also declined. That cost him an additional bit of haranguing, but he shrugged it off.

They took turns napping on shoulders with Maria sleeping more than Dylan. He often teases her about being "solar powered" because her wake/sleep cycle follows the sun. Dylan is more of a night owl, so he filled the time reading her volume of *Fantastic Beasts and Where to Find Them* and thinking.

When he thought she was asleep he gingerly found her hand as it lay next to his. Maria was at that spot where her body was completely asleep with just a corner of her brain awake. She barely registered the touch, but managed to twitch her hand so it fit better, and then she was out. He sat in the dark feeling her hand snuggled in his, her head resting on his shoulder.

He thought about the weekend. It had been time outside of time. Now they were going home, back to other routines and other relationships.

"When we get home," he thought, "if she decides to stay with Benjamin–and that's totally fine–I get that–

they've been together for a really long time. But if she does decide to stay with him, I want to at least have had this." And he caressed her fingers gently with his.

Between games of Werewolf, Schultz hopped forward a few seats to the one across from Dylan and the sleeping Maria. "I thought you said this wasn't a thing," he said.

Dylan shrugged. "It hadn't been. But I think it's gonna be."

Schultz grinned at Dylan, then slid back to his seat for the next game of Werewolf.

When Maria woke up, Dylan wasn't holding her hand. She wasn't sure if the hand-holding had been real or if she had dreamed it. She asked him, "Did you hold my hand while I was sleeping? I thought I felt you take my hand."

Not quite ready to admit to taking her hand he lied. "I was asleep too. I must have grabbed it in my sleep."

As the drowsing cycled throughout the ride home, Dylan took one opportunity to kiss her on the cheek as she was drifting back off, though he knew she wasn't asleep yet.

In telling the story later, Maria said, "I remember that. And then later, I kissed you on the cheek, but you were asleep."

To which Dylan responded, "No I wasn't."

"What?!" Maria exclaimed. "I was sure you were asleep!"

"Nope. Not asleep. Trust me. I was not asleep." He grinned at her.

Dylan dropped Maria off at home at 2am Monday morning. In consideration of their late-night arrival, the school allowed them an excused late start that day. Dylan wasn't going in until he had to, but Maria planned to go in at the regular time to make up an art class assignment. At 7am, I heard Maria's footfalls tumbling down the stairs. She rushed into the dining room with her phone playing Taylor Swift's "Everything Has Changed." Her eyes big as saucers, she held out the phone for me to hear the lyrics:

> 'Cause all I know is we said, "Hello"
> And your eyes look like comin' home
> All I know is a simple name
> And everything has changed
> All I know is you held the door
> You'll be mine and I'll be yours
> All I know since yesterday
> Is everything has changed

I gave her a hug, and she blinked back tears. Her world had shifted seismically. Everything had changed.

Dylan gave Maria a ride home from school and they went for a long walk. They made the decision to officially call off their current relationships. The details of that walk and that conversation are not recorded here, nor should they be. Some moments are intimate and private and belong only to those who live them. This is not reality TV.

I came home from work to find Maria in the living

room recliner, looking a bit of a mess. I let her talk a bit and tell me they decided to break off their current relationships. I reassure her that what she thinks this is, it is.

At one point she kind of laughed through some tears and said, "I need to let Theresa know about Dylan."

I replied, "Well, actually, I've been keeping Sis up-to-date, and I'm sure she's told Tim. Pretty much all the siblings and spouses are up to speed. I talked to Mike and RaDonna last weekend when they were here. Jimmy was in the room when I got that first text and he and Gina live here. We've all been waiting to see how long it was going to take the two of you to figure it out. Katie is standing right here, so she just got updated. You could tell George— he doesn't know yet." I grinned.

To which Maria replied, half annoyed and half laughing, "I'm the youngest in this family. So I'm always the last to know everything because no one ever remembers to tell me anything. Here I am, the last to know again, even when it's my own stuff!"

Benjamin called that night to suggest he and Maria go out for lunch the following afternoon since school dismissed early because of the junior class SAT testing. Maria declined with an excuse and tried to get off the phone quickly. She was planning to wait until after the SAT to tell him they were done. She didn't want him to be thinking about that while trying to concentrate on the test. Benjamin caught her evasive tone and pivoted to asking about Prom. Maria told him she had decided to go to Worlds. He got angry, and told her she needed to correct her priorities. Pushed into a corner, Maria finally said her piece.

Maria came downstairs around 8:00 and said, "Well, it's done. Part of my head is telling me, 'what are you doing??? You've only been talking to Dylan for like 10 days.' But…." She looked at me helplessly.

I hugged her and said, "But your heart knows it's right. And it is right. Nothing would be improved by waiting."

Maria didn't see Benjamin at school the next day because accommodations for her eyes had her taking the SAT in a separate room. They were both spared that encounter.

Like Maria, Dylan didn't want to break up with Natalie, also a junior, right before the SAT, so his breakup waited until Wednesday morning. Natalie didn't have a cell phone and her parents stringently limited their time together outside of school, especially during the week, so an in-school breakup was the only option. Not looking forward to it and wishing there was a more private location, Dylan met up with Natalie in their usual morning spot. It was going to be a bit of a mess, but it had to be done.

Jess came down the hall in time to see Dylan and Natalie obviously in a tough moment. She rounded the corner quickly to where Maria was just leaving her locker. "Don't go that way! Don't go that way! I think Dylan just broke up with Natalie." Maria headed the long way around to their first hour Engineering class.

Maria and Dylan decided not to officially date for a while. High school drama can be intense. It's hard enough to have someone break up with you, and so much worse to watch that person walking around the next day with someone else, or to listen to others commenting on the situation. No need to make things harder than it needed to be for two hurting people they cared about. Dylan and Maria would remain "friends" until after Dylan graduated on May 18. They would keep a distance at school and just see each other outside of school. It helped that there were only two school days left before Easter vacation.

They both blanked out their Facebook relationship status. Maria switched out pictures of her and Benjamin to pictures of her with girlfriends, and Dylan opted for a picture of him standing outside a cave on a Boy Scout spelunking trip. Dylan brought her home from school Thursday and Friday, stayed a bit, then left for his job at the hardware store. Only a few close friends were updated, and most of them were on the Argos team and had watched it happen anyway.

A True True-Love Story

PART V
SPARKS FLY

Sunday, April 14 saw a late spring blizzard, so we were all house-bound. Dylan had worked all day on Saturday and had planned to come over for the day on Sunday, but the blizzard kept him house-bound as well.

Dylan worked full days at the hardware store on Monday and Tuesday of the school's Easter Break week. He came over in the middle of the day on his lunch break, and Maria made sure to have something ready for him. It was his first introduction to her cooking.

She inherited her dad's passion for cooking, and began cooking at a very young age. She requested and received Julia Child's cookbooks for her eighth birthday, and her enthusiastic reaction to receiving a bamboo steamer for Christmas that same year would have gone viral if only we had been filming. Needless to say, Dylan was suitably impressed.

On Wednesday, he had the afternoon off so was able to stay after lunch. They opted to watch *Hitchhiker's Guide to the Galaxy*, a family favorite of ours he had not seen.

Maria said later, "I turned to watch how he would react to something funny that was coming up, and when I leaned forward to look at him, he leaned forward and kissed me, which I wasn't expecting, but OK! Not opposed!"

During those lunch visits, Jimmy had a chance to talk with Dylan, and observe Dylan with Maria. Later he told me, "I've spent more time with Dylan than any of you, and I've actively been paying attention. That's a green light, that's a green light, that's a green light. Mom, I can't even find a yellow light, much less anything that looks like an actual issue. In fact, it's ridiculous how good a fit he is for Maria and the whole family."

A "good fit" who had watched the same family-favorite movies with his own family, enjoyed the same tabletop and RPG gaming, books and nerd pop culture, grew up with incessant wordplay, and spent hours at a grandparent's family farm, closely mimicking Maria's own upbringing. He spoke our family's "language" like a native.

One memorable text conversation during the week was Maria asking Dylan what he had told his friends about her:

> Maria: So what have you told your friends about me?

> Dylan: I don't want to say. You'll get mad at me.

Maria: Ok, well now you have to tell me!

Dylan: I told Michael, "I REALLY like
this girl..........I let her win when
we played Magic. His response
was "Oh sh*t!!!!!!"

He admitted later that his deck had played well against hers, and he had to work really hard not to win that night at the hotel in Missouri. She did legitimately beat him once when they played in Detroit at Worlds.

A True True-Love Story

PART VI
THE KINDLING CATCHES

Months earlier, we had scheduled an Easter vacation college visit to the University of Wisconsin-Milwaukee. Maria had a short list of colleges she wanted to visit her junior year so she would be ready to make a decision early fall of her senior year. By the time Easter vacation came around, it seemed natural to invite Dylan to come along for a day trip together.

April 19, Good Friday, we headed to Milwaukee. We swung by Dylan's house to pick him up around 8am, and he was waiting outside with his mom, Tammy.

We hopped out of my husband's truck to say hello. Dylan introduced Bert and me to his mom. I opted to give her a hug. I figured Dylan might have already told her I hug, and if not, we were going to be family one day, so we may as well start that way.

I could tell she was a little surprised but hugged me back sincerely, and we smiled. I liked her instantly.

Then she stepped up to meet Maria. I wasn't sure how

much she knew at this point, but she greeted Maria a little shyly, and Maria responded in kind. "Hello Maria. It's nice to meet you."

"It's nice to meet you too."

Then they both stood there awkwardly smiling at each other. To which I responded, "Oh, for Pete's sake–give each other a hug too!"

So they did–a bit tentatively on both sides. I could see Maria processing with a "well, that just happened" look on her face. I'm still not sure whether that was the right thing to do, but there it is, part of the story.

Our truck was a large extended cab vehicle that seated 3 in the back row. Before leaving the house, I had told Maria, "Just for the record, it's OK if you sit in the middle seat next to Dylan. In fact, it would be better if you just start out there so you don't have to awkwardly figure out when it's been long enough that you can slide over. Just sit there." She grinned at me and said she'd been thinking the same thing and had been meaning to ask.

So they climbed in the back with Maria in the middle, Dylan behind Bert in the driver's seat, and me riding shotgun. The kids immediately grabbed hands, his right to her left. Then both reached over and grabbed the other hand, his left to her right. They sat that way, fingers entwined, double-hand-holding, for three and a half hours, all the way to Milwaukee. After a couple of hours, near Chicago, I saw Dylan let go with his top outside left hand and stretch his cramping fingers. Maria stretched hers too.

They both rubbed their hands on respective pant legs for a moment, and within 20-30 seconds, re-engaged their outside hands. I never saw them drop the inside handhold or take another stretch break until we got to Milwaukee.

The trip up was uneventful. Dylan had been a little nervous about a long ride with us. Maria had prepared him that there would be lots of talking. I was looking forward to asking all sorts of questions and telling family stories. And then almost no talking happened. Bert had been waiting patiently to share an audiobook with me by Dennis Taylor called *We Are Legion (We Are Bob)*. He started the book as we left town, and we listened and laughed all the way to Milwaukee. It was a fun time, and my questions and stories would wait.

We got to Milwaukee with time to spare before our college visit and spent some time driving around the city, stopping at a game pub restaurant for lunch. It was a fun, college-town kind of place with shelves of games lining the walls and stuffed animals and *Game of Thrones* house banners filling the rafters. We ordered fried cheese curds to share as an appetizer. (We were in Wisconsin–it's mandatory there!) Maria was hungry and ate quite a few, but by the time the entrees arrived her stomach was feeling a bit queasy after all the fried cheese, and she only ate a few bites of her lunch.

We still had some extra time, so we found our way to the UWM Student Center. Maria and Dylan took themselves on a tour of the place while Bert and I enjoyed the college ambiance by ourselves, reminiscing through some of our old college stories.

When the kids got back from their walkabout, we headed over to Visitor Orientation. We sat through the promotional slideshow then headed out for the campus tour. Walking around campus holding hands, Maria and Dylan were both taking it in. Dylan said later that he was paranoid about saying something that would influence her decision.

"I wanted to be supportive of wherever she wanted to go. I thought UWM looked like a cool place, but I also knew that would make things 'interesting' for working things out, since I was still going to be in Peoria at Bradley University. I wasn't concerned if that happened. It would just make things more complicated."

About halfway through the tour, we got to the library. It was uncomfortably warm in the building, and the tour stopped near the Circulation Desk while the tour guide talked at length about the building's history and namesake. When it was finally time to move on, Maria took one step, wobbled hard, and nearly fell. She dropped down to her knees and slid into a sitting position.

Pale as a ghost, she looked up and said, "Everything sounds funny, and I can't see very well."

We got her jacket off, gave her a water bottle, and fanned her. We sent the group on without us and waited for the dizzy spell to pass. We surmised that she must have nearly passed out from locking her knees during the guide's long-winded description.

After about 10 minutes on the floor, we all decided fresh air would help. I helped Maria up and out the door Dylan held for us. We found a bench nearby and sat down, backs to the sun, now a bit low in the sky. We sat for about half an hour trying to decide our next steps. I asked her "Do you want to go here?"

"No." She replied.

"Do you want to go home?"

"Yes."

Dylan said later he was very relieved to hear her say she didn't want to go to UWM. While he didn't want her to choose her college because of him, he also very much hoped her college would be closer to his than Milwaukee.

We collectively decided to call it enough and head home. Maria made the walk back to the parking deck without issue.

On the ride home, we stopped at a favorite cheese and trinket shop, The Mouse House. We got some cheese, snacks, and ice cream. The kids sat in the back eating ice cream, and we told some family stories and enjoyed the company.

An hour down the road, the ice cream was long finished, and Maria and Dylan had settled in with her head on his chest and her arm across him while he supported her elbow with his hand and rested his head on the top of hers. Both were sound asleep.

I have a picture. ☺

After a nap, Dylan woke up, but Maria continued to sleep for the entire ride home. Dylan said later it was a very sore ride. "Can't move. Don't want to wake her up. Breathe. Breathe. Breathe. Tiny shift. That's a little better." He held Maria asleep across his chest for hours, passing the time looking thoughtfully out the window, gazing at Maria as she slept, and occasionally closing his eyes to doze himself.

By the time we got home after dropping Dylan home, Maria was running a 101.5 fever. By Saturday morning, it was well over 103. She didn't feel terrible, just exhausted with a headache from the fever. Nothing intestinal, which helped. She mostly slept.

Jimmy and Gina's kids had been sick earlier in the week, so Maria's sister and brother-in-law, Theresa and Tim, had already decided to stay in Wisconsin and have Easter with Tim's parents. With Maria sick, George and his wife, Katie, also opted out of Easter with us, and changed plans to only go to Katie's parents. It had been a long winter of sick kids and no one wanted to risk one more bug. We had a family gathering planned the following weekend for Bert's 60th birthday party anyway. Everyone meeting Dylan would wait a week.

April 21, Easter Sunday, Maria's fever was still over 103. Tylenol barely touched it. Dylan figured he was as exposed as he could get and came over in the early afternoon after having Easter with his family. He stopped first at the local Kroger's grocery store to get her flowers.

While there, he considered buying her some chicken soup. It seemed appropriate, he said later, but bringing canned soup just seemed sad after experiencing her cooking. So he opted for just flowers.

Easter Sunday breakfast at The Farm is generally a large affair, and missing 7 people barely made a dent. Maria's Grandpa, 2 grandmas, 3 aunts and uncles, 2 cousins with kids, her brother Mike and his wife RaDonna (who braved the bug) with their 2 kids, and a few other people made for a group of about 25.

Dylan arrived to find the circle drive full of cars, so he had to park a fair distance away. I was inside with Maria who was sitting in the recliner in the living room. Through the front window I saw his car pull up. Maria couldn't see from where she was sitting, and I decided to let him surprise her. She knew he was coming, but not when.

As Dylan stepped out of his car with a vase in his hand, I had a moment of melt followed by a moment of empathy. Most of the family was outside on the porch, and he was about to run something of a gauntlet past that crowd he had never met to bring his new girlfriend flowers.

He marched firmly up the gravel drive, up the sidewalk, and said hello to those nearby as he stepped up onto the porch. Bert greeted him, introduced him to a few people–I'm certain Dylan has no recollection of the introductions–and told him to go on inside, Maria was waiting. Though Dylan had already learned he was welcome to come inside without waiting for someone to open the door, he hesitated in front of all those people. As he processed his options and weighed the appropriate behavior in slow motion, Bert repeated to go on inside, and added that Maria was just inside the door. Dylan's hand reached the handle, but he moved no farther, still processing proper protocol. It took a third comment from Bert before he opened the door and walked in.

Maria's eyes lit up when she saw him. "You brought me flowers!" she exclaimed, and his face visibly relaxed as he smiled back at her. Then things got awkward. Since she was sitting in a recliner, they couldn't exactly hug, and kissing didn't seem appropriate either. So he just stood there, right inside the door, holding her flowers, and they continued to smile broadly at each other.

Finally, I laughed and said, "It's OK to kiss her hello!"

He grinned self-consciously at me but accepted the permission. He leaned in but only made contact with the top of Maria's head as she looked down in embarrassment. At that point I figured it was past time for me to make an exit and give them a few minutes together.

Those were the first flowers a boy had given her, and Maria still has the little "Happy Easter" stick that was in them.

Dylan said later the atmosphere, including the gathering of family outside and a large cornucopia of fresh fruit and Peeps on the dining room table, felt familiar and comfortable. It reminded him very much of his own extended family Easter gatherings.

PART VII
THE KINDLING EXPLODES

Easter break continued into Monday, a convenience considering Maria's fever continued to be over 102 degrees. The FIRST Robotics team was leaving Wednesday for Worlds in Detroit, and Maria was running out of time to get better in time for the trip.

We visited PromptCare to be sure there wasn't any infection that antibiotics could help, and were told the virus going around was taking 4 days of fever to clear. Tuesday should be the end of it.

Dylan worked all day and didn't stop over, though the usual texting was going on in the background. They were both getting seriously concerned she wouldn't be well soon enough to go to Worlds, which they both agreed would just be a sorry state of affairs.

She was still running a high fever on Tuesday morning, and Dylan had a sad day at school without her. By early afternoon, her fever dropped down to 101; by evening, down to 99. Finally!

Although technically in violation of school health rules requiring 24 hours fever-free before returning to class, her temp was normal Wednesday morning, and she went to school, feeling mostly recovered. She was not missing Worlds. We were going to Worlds as well, so if there was any kind of highly unlikely relapse, we would be close by.

At school for just one day, Maria picked up homework assignments for the previous day plus Thursday and Friday to take with her to Detroit. I was dubious about the value of taking homework along, but my little Valedictorian was adamant. She might not work on it, but she wanted the option if a window presented itself. Dylan brought her home after school to grab her packed bag, then they headed over to the school parking lot to wait for the bus.

They were so excited! "YAY! She's better!!!! We get to GO!!!!!"

Sitting in his car waiting for bus-loading to be announced, Maria leaned over and gave him a kiss. Later, she said, "Mom, it was just a kiss–I mean not a kiss, just a little peck." But timing is everything. Her little kiss landed just as Mr. Walser walked up to tell them they could start loading the bus.

Oblivious in their own world, they hadn't seen him walk up. He knocked on the driver's window, startling them. With a roll of his eyes he said, "Na-uh. None of that. I don't care what you do in this car, but when you get on that bus until you get back on Saturday night, there will be no kissing, no hand holding, and no hugging. You will sit in separate seats, and I want to see 12 inches of daylight between you at all times. I expect you to act professionally at Worlds."

Dang it! So much for a repeat of the bus ride to Missouri. Separate seats on a six-and-a-half hour bus ride. Twelve inches of daylight. For 4 days they couldn't do anything besides talk and tease and make eyes at each other.

Getting on the bus they sat directly across from each other and "held" feet in the aisle: one on top of the other, or snuggled one foot up next to the others. That wasn't a sustainable posture, though, and after a while they un-crooked themselves and sat straight. Dylan played on his phone while Maria actually did pull out her Algebra textbook and worked on homework.

At the lunch stop at Culver's, everyone got a stretch break. As the kids piled out of the bus and flooded into the building, Dylan and Maria stepped to the side to let the horde pass. A moment to stand close to each other.

Once inside, they walked together to the edge of the counter, and Dylan leaned into Maria's ear to read her the menu over the bedlam. Mr. Walzer was standing at the back of the crowd keeping a watchful eye on everyone. He told me later he noticed what Dylan was doing and the casual familiarity of their manner. His comment to himself was, "Wow, she trained him fast!" In fact, they never discussed her need to have someone read the menu, and she didn't ask him to do it. It was just part of their connectedness that he reflexively read it to her as though he'd been doing it all his life.

There was some discussion of favorite ice cream flavors. Both agreed on strawberry but disagreed about caramel. They ordered. She got a chocolate custard Concrete Mixer with caramel and brownies; he got a strawberry milkshake, and they got duplicate orders of cheese curds.

They headed to a small, 4-person table near the back where Chad and Caleb were already seated. Sitting close to each other in the small space, Dylan and Maria entangled ankles under the table. Dylan removed only half the paper wrapper from his straw and set the straw in his mouth, casually pointing the still-covered end in her general direction. At an opportune moment, he puffed air through the straw, shooting her squarely on the cheek with the paper. He grinned at her startled exclamation and her jump.

Chad and Caleb gave them both some good-natured grief about being cute and "couple-y." Maria and Dylan good-naturedly ignored them and enjoyed their few minutes of close contact.

Back on the bus they resumed separate seats across from each other. Energized after the lunch break, the bus got louder with kids talking and laughing to pass the time. Ever ready to sing, Maria and Brendan belted out renditions of "Where Is My Hairbrush," "The Pirates Who

Don't Do Anything," and "Barbara Manatee," among other classics from "Silly Songs with Larry" from the Veggie Tales videos they had both watched when they were little. Other bus antics included Maria creating "unicorn horns" for several of the guys using the wristful of hair ties she always had on her. Brendan, particularly enthusiastic about silliness, left his in all day, with the tiny "horn" from his super-short hair poking out from the front of his turned-backwards ball cap.

In the Pits at the competition, Maria and Dylan were restricted to old-fashioned courtship. Maria kept calling him sweet and throwing hotel restaurant sugar packets at him, reprising their first breakfast at McDonald's. When she wasn't looking, he would sneak candy wrappers into her pockets, into her shoes, into her hair. She did the same, but couldn't match his level of finesse; he could probably moonlight as a pickpocket! But he had a lot of pockets for her to pick from in those bumble bee yellow-striped cargo pants, so she managed some successes.

They agreed it would be best if they kept their hands in their own pockets as much as possible to avoid inadvertently breaking the ban on hand-holding. They only ignored the ban for the brief moments when they were out of view in the tunnel exiting the Pit area. And they continued "holding" crisscrossed feet under the table at lunchtime.

A tradition at FIRST Robotics competitions is for each team to bring a memento to hand out to other teams. For example, Argos brought a dog food bowl of stickers. The method of distribution left a mystery about who gave out what, so Maria and Dylan didn't know which team gave out the 2-inch plastic babies. Whatever. The baby became one of the more popular items for Dylan to reverse-pick-pocket into Argos team member's cargo pants. Maria kept the plastic baby at the end of the competition, and it sits on her curio shelf along with the original McDonald's sugar packet.

Dylan and Maria spent the days happily in each other's company while, of course, observing 12 inches of daylight as required. They shared the intensity and adrenaline of the competition and enjoyed the downtime between matches together. As the team left the Arena each night, Maria and Dylan hung to the back of the pack and held pinkies while the whole group wandered around looking for the bus.

At dinner in the hotel conference room, they sat together with the now-familiar entwined ankles, and contraband pinkie holds under the table. After they finished eating, Brendan, Dylan, and Maria went back to hotel rooms, grabbed Magic decks and met back in the lobby to play a game or two before curfew. They all brought swimsuits, but never had enough time to be worth getting in a pool. There was no opportunity for stolen kisses–that would have been a higher magnitude of trouble than either of them was willing to risk. But there were hugs in the elevator going up to their respective rooms each night. Which, according to Maria, was just fantastic, with contact limited such as it was.

The robotics matches went well and not so well, and they finished in the middle of the standings. But the team was still selected as part of an Alliance for the Finals. The online videos of the matches are full of drama and competition not recorded here. They're worth the watch.

In the finals of their division, their Alliance was finally beaten, and it was time to go home.

On the bus ride back, they again sat across from each other talking, knees touching in the aisle. Someone was playing Billy Joel songs, and Maria sang softly to Dylan. After nightfall, in the dark monotony of the long ride, they defiantly entwined their fingers and actively held hands for the first time since Wednesday. At one point, Dylan leaned across the aisle and gave her a kiss on the cheek.

Finally back to Bartonville, the bus received a celebratory police escort back to the high school. Dylan dropped Maria home, both of them exhausted, at 2am Sunday morning.

Sunday April 28 brought another full day after a full week. Bert's 60th birthday party was that afternoon. Theresa and Tim came down from Wisconsin to join extended family in our commercial building that is part game company storage and part party space. Maria and Dylan had been looking forward to introducing him to both The Center and her family at the party. Maria was scheduled for induction into the National Honor Society before the party, and Dylan was unavailable afterwards because he was joining his family to see Avengers: Endgame in the evening. After all the restrictions since Wednesday, Maria and Dylan didn't see each other at all on Sunday.

Monday brought their self-imposed restriction to keeping a distance at school. It was getting tiresome. They were not, they continued to tell everyone, dating. They did not sit close or hold hands, except a light pinky hold when they got to the back hallway on their way to first hour Engineering. They were limited to a few minutes together after school until Dylan went to work and texting after he got home. Maria was buried with school work. She was stressed trying to catch up from missing so many days, end-of-year band and choir performances, and auditions for her senior year placements. They got through it.

Friday May 3 brought a very special occasion. Limestone high school has an end-of-year event called And All That Jazz… It includes performances by the jazz band and jazz choir ensembles, and a fancy meal created as part of the final semester project by the Quantity Foods class. In the cafeteria, rented round tables replaced the high school's institutional rectangular cafeteria tables. They were arranged to create a central dance floor, and were set with tablecloths, candles, and edible centerpieces. Maria was to perform as a member of the Melodettes jazz choir. We had purchased a table of eight and had a ticket for Dylan. At the last, we had someone cancel so had an extra ticket for Dylan's mom, Tammy, who had been very involved in band when she was in high school. She was super excited for the ticket. She had only seen Maria once, that one brief encounter before the trip to Milwaukee.

Maria could not have looked more beautiful. The dress the Melodettes had that year suited her figure perfectly, and its dark blue color accentuated her already intensely blue eyes. Later Maria showed me a couple of texts Dylan sent her that evening. "That dress...you look MIND-BLOWINGLY GORGEOUS!!!!!" and "It was so much more amazing to see and hear you sing than I ever could have imagined. I just wanted to point you out to everyone in the room–that one, that one right there, SHE'S MINE!!!"

I had left my seat to talk with a friend, so when Maria joined us at the table after her performance, she took my empty chair. We hadn't thought of leaving a seat at the table for her. When I returned, I knelt on the floor between Maria and Tammy, chatting with both. Dylan was on the other side of his mom. He leaned forward, and offered intensely that he was willing to let me have his chair. I considered saying I was fine, when he said, "No, really, I'd be happy to switch with you!" I agreed to switch, and as he jumped out of his chair to kneel where I had been beside Maria, I realized he wasn't just politely giving up his seat to the older adult. I can be a bit dense sometimes.

The next song was a slow jazz piece, and Maria smiled

at him to dance with her. They had discussed this before the event. He didn't dance, but depending on how the night went, he might be willing. He followed her out to the dance floor just a few steps away from where she had been sitting. That first dance was precious to watch. I have a picture.

When they came back to the table 4 songs later, I told him he did just fine. He laughed and said, "I was fine as long as I was looking right into her eyes. Any time I looked away I would stumble. Once I stepped on her foot, and once I stepped on my own. So I decided I should just maintain eye contact. It would be safer for both of us that way."

PART VIII
THE LOGS CATCH

The next day they went on their first actual date to see Avengers: Endgame at the AMC theatre in Pekin. Dylan had already seen it the week before with his family, so he knew how it ended. Maria did not and bawled at the closing. Throughout the movie, the character Thanos repeats the line, "I–am–inevitable." Each time, Dylan leaned over and dramatically intoned, "I–am–a vegetable," insisting Thanos's coloring was reminiscent of an eggplant. She tried really hard not to laugh because it was always at very dramatic parts in the movie, but she mostly failed as being together just made her happy.

On Sunday, Dylan stopped over, and I happened to be sitting in the living room while Maria and Dylan were on the front porch swing. Her phone was playing her radio station, and Ed Sheeran's song, "Perfect" came on. She sang it for Dylan.

I found a love for me
Darling just dive right in and follow my lead
Well I found a girl beautiful and sweet
I never knew you were the someone waiting for me

'Cause we were just kids when we fell in love
Not knowing what it was
I will not give you up this time
But darling, just kiss me slow, your heart is all I own
And in your eyes you're holding mine

Baby, I'm dancing in the dark with you between
*   my arms*
Barefoot on the grass, listening to our favorite song
When you said you looked a mess, I whispered
*   underneath my breath*
But you heard it, darling, you look perfect tonight

Well I found a woman, stronger than anyone I know
She shares my dreams, I hope that someday I'll share
*   her home*
I found a love, to carry more than just my secrets
To carry love, to carry children of our own

We are still kids, but we're so in love
Fighting against all odds
I know we'll be alright this time
Darling, just hold my hand

71

Be my girl, I'll be your man
I see my future in your eyes

Baby, I'm dancing in the dark, with you between
   my arms
Barefoot on the grass, listening to our favorite song
When I saw you in that dress, looking so beautiful
I don't deserve this, darling, you look perfect tonight

Baby, I'm dancing in the dark, with you between
   my arms
Barefoot on the grass, listening to our favorite song
I have faith in what I see
Now I know I have met an angel in person
And she looks perfect
I don't deserve this
You look perfect tonight

Watching the emotions play out on both their faces as she sang was exquisite. It was a beautiful moment I felt privileged to witness.

Monday brought the school week back around with their continued policy of restraint. Maria was still trying to get caught up and study for finals and Dylan was only a week from graduation. They were both ready for the school year to be over. On Wednesday, May 8, they took their first selfie together at our house. They agreed it was past time to have a couple's picture for themselves.

Friday, May 10, was an early dismissal day at school, so Maria and Dylan decided to go to Thanh Linh for the lunch buffet. Chad was initially planning to go as well, but opted out at the last minute, so they went just the two of them.

At 4:15pm I got a text from Maria. It said, "We are officially dating as of a few hours ago. We went to Thanh Linh and the fortune cookies were taunting us." The text included a screenshot of the fortune cookies. Hers said, "You will be fortunate if you accept the next proposition you hear." His said, "Your present plans are going to succeed." They just called it done.

Around 7pm, I received a text from a friend that said, "It's Facebook official!" with a screenshot of Maria's updated Facebook page. It said, "In a Relationship with Dylan Livingston."

I sent her back, "Been waiting for that since March 28! Why do I feel like she just got engaged?!" and I made the same comment to Bert.

He agreed and added, "That was the 'yes' that actually mattered. That one begins their journey. The next one will be just another step on the road."

And so it began. Until death do they part.

ADDENDUM

"Their" song is "Love Like Crazy" by Lee Brice. For a class assignment in March 2020, Maria made a video of their first year together with this song as the background. It's available on YouTube.

> *They called them crazy when they started out*
> *Said seventeen's too young to know what loves about*
> *They've been together fifty-eight years now*
> *That's crazy*
>
> *He brought home sixty-seven bucks a week*
> *He bought a little two-bedroom house on*
>   *Maple Street*
> *Where she blessed him with six more mouths to feed*
> *Yea that's crazy*
>
> *Just ask him how he did it, he'll say pull up a seat*
> *It'll only take a minute, to tell you everything*
> *Be a best friend, tell the truth, and overuse I love you*
> *Go to work, do your best, don't outsmart your*
>   *common sense*
> *Never let your prayin' knees get lazy*
> *And love like crazy*

They called him crazy when he quit his job
Said them home computers, boy they'll never take off
He sold his one man shop to Microsoft
And they paid like crazy

Just ask him how he made it
He'll tell you faith and sweat
And the heart of a faithful woman,
Who never let him forget

Be a best friend, tell the truth, and overuse I love you
Go to work, do your best, don't outsmart your
      common sense
Never let your prayin' knees get lazy
And love like crazy

Always treat your woman like a lady
Never get to old to call her baby
Never let your prayin' knees get lazy
And love like crazy

They called him crazy when they started out
They've been together fifty-eight years now

Ain't that crazy?

FEAR(LESS)

By Maria Sanders, at age 16, on March 3, 2019, three weeks before she and Dylan connected.

I have a rare affliction,
One you can hardly see.
But it did crash around my head
With unexpected glee.

Before I could even breathe
My fate was etched in stone.
The dice already cast
For a game I would play alone.

My vision becomes poorer
With every rising sun.
One day I will be blind,
My malady will have won.

I was 13 when I got the news;
It gave me such a fright.
I knew not what to do;
How do you cope with such a plight?

I feared for the future.
I feared for my dreams.

I dared not hope
Things were better than they seemed.

I was young,
Untried.
Unsure of who to be.
And faced with a challenge
I'd once before seen.

Somewhere in the panic,
Somewhere in the strife.
A very young lady
Found her purpose in life.

I found who I was;
I found who I am;
I found a truth about life
That few understand.

You decide your future.
You decide your fate.
Perception is everything,
Something you get to make.

I chose to be happy.
I chose to move on.
I chose to make a tragedy
Just one note in the song.

DYLAN'S GRADUATION LETTER FROM ME

May 18, 2019

Dear Dylan,

Congrats on your graduation!

Instead of buying greeting cards, spending $8 and 2 hours to find one that kind of says what I want, a few years back I started writing letters instead. So here goes–what I would say to you if we had a minute and I could find the words in the moment.

MARIA ELIZABETH SANDERS IS YOUR GIRLFRIEND!!!! YOURS! SHE SAID YES!!! AT LONG LAST, IT'S OFFICIAL!!!!

:D :D :D :D :D

You are an amazing young man–the person I thought Maria would have to leave Limestone and Bartonville to find. And here you are–just a couple miles down the road, all this time. But timing is everything–I trust that you met in perfect timing, just when you were both ready.

After the older 4 were married, there have been many jesting (and not exactly jesting :D) conversations about who Maria would bring to the family, and how everyone else brought someone that was a good fit to the whole group, so the bar was set really high. They joked that they had the authority to tell her 'no' if she brought someone they didn't like. We are all 10 of us (4 adult children with spouses, plus Bert and I) completely on board with this. She did good. Better than good. You exceed all reasonable expectations, and even our unreasonable expectations for the person we hoped she would find. In Jimmy's words, "I've spent more time with Dylan than any of you, and I've actively been paying attention. That's a green light, that's a green light, that's a green light. Mom, I can't even find a yellow light, much less anything that looks like an actual issue. In fact, it's ridiculous how good a fit he is, for Maria and the whole family."

I look at Maria and I look at how you perceive yourself, and I think there is a part of you standing in awe. Me?! I get to have and to hold this incredible being? This breathtakingly beautiful, intelligent, witty, kind, gentle soul loves me? How does that even happen? If you had made a list of everything you wanted, you would have left a few things off. It would have been unreasonable to ask God/Fates/Universe to supply you with someone who was everything. But she is. Everything and then some. We've wondered who would come along to possibly match that. Hoping she didn't settle for someone who was just "good enough." You are more than "good enough." You "exceed specs." You deserve her.

You are her intellectual equal, even a little ahead. That's hard to do at her level, but more important than you understand right now.

You have a wonderful sense of humor. She and her dad do love their wordplay.

You are kind and gentle. Maria has learned to manage her anxiety, but glows under a gentle touch.

You are strong. She needs someone she can trust and to take the lead. She is after all, a very youngest. Don't be afraid to be her protector, or to pull her forward to new experiences and stretch her self-imposed boundaries. Like playing Dodge Ball. :D

You aren't intimidated by her. She has strength and wisdom beyond her years. She is extraordinary. She is not like anyone you've ever met. Not like anyone else at Limestone or Oak Grove. Everyone likes her, but no one has been like her. Until you.

You aren't emotionally broken. Neither is she.

You work really hard. You have direction and will be able to support your family.

You know the cultural references she's grown up with. You have a shared history you didn't know you were sharing while you both grew up.

You share her love of nature. Nature is her home and her happy place. Where she finds peace and contentment. Respite from stress and Life; a centering for her soul.

She wants children. She was just short of 3–less than Melany's age–when RaDonna first came to the family, and the other in-laws came soon after. She really grew up with 8 siblings, not 4. Although the age gap makes them more like aunts and uncles than true siblings, except George and Katie. Plus of course all the nieces and nephews. Plus all the actual aunts, uncles, cousins, friends who would show up at The Farm at all times of day and days of the week. She has been raised in a busy house full of life and full of family. It's the life she's known and the life she wants. I know so many in your generation who want few or no children, even sterilizing themselves in their early twenties. Sterile is such a sad, lifeless word. They really don't understand what they're choosing, but our culture has taught that children are messy, expensive, and more work than they are worth. That she could find someone who has not absorbed that message, and instead values family and children—that is a rare thing in our culture today.

You love her. And she, you. You are connected from your entwined fingers to your entwined souls. And two shall become one. Someday you'll absolutely drive each other crazy, probably won't like each other, will be disappointed in each other, wonder if it was a mistake, and work to remember the magic of this beginning. I'm glad you will have magic to remember.

Sitting back with popcorn, watching your movie, transported back to my own magical beginnings with my husband. While the plotline will be different, I hope your "happily ever after" will be the same. ("Ever after" means, "after 50." Between where you are and where I am is a whole lot of messy! LOL!!!)

PHOTO ALBUM

"She was also quite beautiful. She had waist-length chocolate brown hair, intensely blue eyes, and she dressed with an iconic self-assured style unlike anyone else at the high school." (Prologue)

Her extensive wardrobe came exclusively from hand-me-downs and Goodwill Industries, put together in combinations using her own sense of style.

Dylan and Maria

OPPOSITE PAGE
November 12, 2018
Maria wearing her Melodettes dress that was the subject
of Dylan's text at And All That Jazz… (Part VII)

...

November 10, 2018, Design and Competition day
Maria explaining her team's "dustpan" design. I didn't
know who Dylan was and didn't take any pictures of the
random kid named Dylan who explained the other team's
design.

Dylan and Maria

A view of the opposing design. Maria was nervous that her teams' simple "dustpan" design would be no match for the competition.

Maria is wearing her Legends of Draxia by Mythica Gaming t-shirt (shameless plug for her brother's game and game company).

March 19, 2019
Fashion Shame (Part I)

March 23, 2019
Central Illinois Regional
at Bradley University, Peoria IL (Part I)

Post awards ceremony decompress: I was taking pictures of Maria. I didn't know I was also photographing my future son-in-law, though I was observing their interaction. They had no idea their worlds were about to collide, only that CIR was so much fun…

April 6, 2019
Central Missouri Regional
in Sedalia MO (Part IV)

Perching

Mutual angst over the broken robot

Dylan and Maria

April 18, 2019

Heading back from University of Wisconsin–Milwaukee, three weeks after that first car ride home. (I told you I had a picture. ☺)

At the time I didn't register the pallor of Maria's face which is so obvious in this picture–an indication she was getting ill. (Part V)

April 25, 2019
First Robotics Worlds
in Detroit MI (Part VII)

Courting

April 26, 2019

Keeping hands in pockets

Dylan and Maria

OPPOSITE PAGE
May 8, 2019
First couple selfie

...

May 18, 2019
Dylan's Graduation

Dylan and Maria

May 10, 2019
Thahn Lihns right after Dylan officially asked her to be his girlfriend.

His Fortune Cookie:

Your present plans are going to succeed.

Lucky # 7, 20, 33, 49, 2, 22
Learn Chinese: To compare. Bi 比

Her Fortune Cookie:

You will be fortunate, if you accept the next proposition you hear.
Lucky # 5, 18, 39, 43, 59, 30
Learn Chinese: Heavy, Zhong 重

October 2019

Returning from Chicago Lighthouse for the Blind/Pangere Center. The appointment included an official designation as legally blind. Maria is wearing the soldered heart Dylan made her.

2020
One year anniversary

Dylan and Maria

May 28, 2022
Save the Date

May 28, 2022
Two Shall Become One

www.ingramcontent.com/pod-product-compliance
Lightning Source LLC
Chambersburg PA
CBHW071021120626
46546CB00003B/1184